The Drunken Boat

& Other Poems From The French Of Arthur Rimbaud

Bi-lingual Edition

American Versions By Eric Greinke

Also By Eric Greinke

*Sand & Other Poems**
*Caged Angels**
10 Michigan Poets (as Editor)*
*The Last Ballet**
*Iron Rose**
Masterpiece Theater (with Brian Adam)*
*The Broken Lock (Selected Poems 1960-1975)**
The Art of Natural Fishing
Whole Self / Whole World (*Quality of Life in
        the 21st Century*)
Sea Dog (*A Coast Guard Memoir*)
Selected Poems 1972-2005

* Out of print

The Drunken Boat

& Other Poems From The
French Of Arthur Rimbaud

American Versions By Eric Greinke

PRESA :S: PRESS

Copyright © 2007 Eric Greinke

Acknowledgments

The first two editions of these translations were published by Free Books, Inc., Grand Rapids, Michigan, copyright 1975, 1976, Eric Greinke. *The Bridges* first appeared in *Big Scream*, a literary journal, in 1976. The third edition was published by Presa Press in 2005. *The Drunken Boat* was published in a bi-lingual presentation in *Big Scream*, 2006. The author is grateful to the following individuals for their support: Robert Bly, David Cope, Ronnie M. Lane, Roseanne Ritzema & Leslie H. Whitten, Jr..

Fourth Edition

PRINTED IN THE UNITED STATES OF AMERICA

ISBN: 0-9772524-7-7

Library of Congress Control Number: 2007920088

Cataloging Information: 1. Greinke, Eric, 1948- .
2. Poetry. 3. Translation.

PRESA :S: PRESS

PO Box 792, Rockford MI 49341
presapress@aol.com   www.presapress.com

Table Of Contents

* First publication this edition.

Introduction To The Fourth Edition

Rimbaud's poetic act is so iconic that scholars have taken decades to separate the reality from the legend. His own brother-in-law perpetrated the myth of the mystical Rimbaud, born with his eyes open, crawling toward the door, a natural poetic genius, bursting on the Parisian literary scene full-blown, to mock the great poets of his time & seduce Paul Verlaine into a toxic relationship that ended with a bullet & a dramatic extended prose poem (*A Season In Hell*) as an amazing farewell to literature, the young poet never writing again after his teenage years, eventually dying young in Africa, a gun-runner & slave trader.

While there is a core of truth to this long-standing myth, the actual facts are significantly different, & perhaps more interesting.

Rimbaud was born on October 20, 1854, in a small rural town in the north of France. He was a gifted child & an early reader. His father left the family when Arthur was four, leaving him to deal with a domineering mother. He was given to wild pranks & his mother had a difficult time bending him to her will. His relationship with his mother was clearly antagonistic. His nickname for her was "the mouth of darkness." His letters contain many references to their conflicts.

He skipped grades in school & attended

college at the age of eleven. He was so gifted that he continued to skip grades in college.

Rimbaudian scholar Wyatt Mason asserts that "Rimbaud made himself a poet by a long, involved, and sober study of the history of poetry." Rimbaud was a voracious reader who was very well versed in the contemporary poetry of his day. Many of his early letters contain literary criticism of new collections of poetry. They also reflect a constant search for new books. His letters to his teacher Georges Izambard were primarily pleas for various books that he couldn't get in Roche.

At the age of fourteen, he won a first prize at the Concours Académique. He received numerous prizes for his first poems. After graduation, in 1870, he made several attempts to run away from home. He sent letters to several of the leading Parisian poets, trying to get a sponsor for his campaign. He had prepared for his assault on Paris like a general, hoping to storm the academy & bowl them over with his talent. He finally received an invitation from poet Paul Verlaine, to whom he'd sent poems & a plea for help. Verlaine recognized the revolutionary value of Rimbaud's poetry, & became his chief sponsor & supporter among the Parisian poets.

Rimbaud wrote satires of the established older poets, mocking their styles in sequences such as *Old Coppées* & *Album Called "Zutique."*

He engaged in drunken adolescent behavior & continued his proclivity toward practical jokes & pranks among the poets. Understandably, they failed to take him as seriously as he wanted them to. He traveled extensively throughout Europe with Verlaine, to the consternation of Verlaine's wife & family. Finally, during a quarrel in which Rimbaud threatened to leave him, Verlaine shot Rimbaud through the hand, & ended up in prison for the next two years for the deed.

A Season In Hell was not Rimbaud's final farewell to literature as the myth would have it. It was self published by Rimbaud in 1873 in an edition of five hundred copies. Rimbaud left most of the books at the printers, & they were discovered by Leon Losseau in the attic of M. J. Poot & Co. (the printers) in 1901, but not made public until 1910. By then, the myth had shoes. An analogy would be the myth that Vikings wore horned helmets. They didn't, but the image persists to this day in popular culture.

The evidence is that he actually continued to write a heightened form of prose poem, known as *Illuminations,* for another two years after *A Season in Hell* - to finally quit poetry at the age of twenty-one. This explains why the *Illuminations* are his most complex & progressive works. They were actually his last.

Wyatt Mason debunks the accumulated myths about Rimbaud in his book *I Promise To Be Good - The Letters of Arthur Rimbaud* (Modern Library, 2003).

I first became aware of the visionary works of the poetic genius Arthur Rimbaud in a round-about

9

way. As an undergraduate English major I had completed a triple major in American Literature, English Literature & Creative Writing, taking all my electives in my majors & immersing myself in English-language literature, but I hadn't studied French literature. Since 1968, I had published my poems in little literary magazines, & several books & chapbooks, years before I became aware of Rimbaud. In 1972, several critics, in reviewing my poetry, compared me to him.

Intrigued, I picked up the New Directions books by Louise Varese, considered at the time to be the standard Rimbaud translations in bi-lingual editions. As I read Rimbaud for the first time, two things happened.

First, I experienced a strong feeling of familiarity & recognition, commonly referred to as déjà vu. I felt that I had *dreamt* those poems before I ever read them. As irrational as it seems, I couldn't shake the feeling that I had written them myself in another life. I am not a believer in reincarnation or past lives, but the feeling has persisted for over thirty years, & I can no longer question it, even at the risk of embarrassing myself with sane society.

The other feeling I had upon discovering Rimbaud for the first time, was *indignation*. Armed with high school French & a dictionary, I read the originals of the poems, & was shocked to see that the translator had distorted them almost beyond recognition. I sought out other versions, & was disgusted to find that none of the popular English

10

translations were good. The professors of French literature had turned the poetry of France's greatest poet into *bad prose*, with the musical & painterly qualities removed. To add insult to injury, they were also inaccurate imagistically. The tone was wrong, too. They had taken out much of the adolescent exuberance, the keen persona, & the *feeling*. They were too literal to be literate.

Rimbaud, perhaps more than most poets, may best be translated by another poet, rather than a language professor. Ninety-five percent professor & five percent poet doesn't cut it. Translators of poetry must be ninety-five percent poet & five percent linguist. This is especially true of Rimbaud, who often used symbols, images & persona ironically.

Rimbaud's work has been rendered nearly incomprehensible by mistranslation by non-poet scholars. They are at a disadvantage & they pass that disadvantage on to unsuspecting readers. Rimbaud's frequent use of ironic imagery made his poetry difficult in his own day, & some of his references have lost their grounding in the vernacular of his times, but the images may be reanimated by recognizing the tone & ideation of the original. Restoring the surface qualities has, therefore, been one of my goals. The meaning emerges when the tone & persona are restored.

The first poem I translated was Rimbaud's greatest, *The Drunken Boat*. I was in love! The poem is amazing in so many ways. Historically, it was one of Rimbaud's earliest works, probably written in 1871 at the age of sixteen or seventeen. He arrived in Paris for his first visit with Paul Verlaine in September of 1871, *Le Bateau ivre* in hand.

The Drunken Boat is the best example of an extended metaphor in literature. It also disproves the general assumption that lyric poems must be short. It booms, whispers, cries, laughs, a *tour de force*. In the French, it is one long symphonic tone poem.

It has often been said that in the translation of poetry, the music is the first thing to go. Restoring the music to *The Drunken Boat* was my initial goal. My version rolls off the tongue & sounds like music when read aloud.

Rimbaud pushed the envelope of poetry in many ways. He was multi-seminal, uninhibited, & a verbal savant. His choices of personae, forms & styles were wide-ranging & probably mostly intuitive. A translator is faced with *many potential synonyms* when translating from one language to another, & herein lies the element of poetic choice & persona. A literal translation is *never* possible, because of the existence of multiple synonyms in both languages. In many ways, a translation is a new poem, inspired & modeled on the original.

I want to assert that the choice between synonyms must be made based on *poetic value*. While some may cry "foul!" at the choice of, say, "car" instead of "carriage" (in *A Winter Dream*), such an interpretation is much more consistent with the timeless, bright, energetic, adolescent, almost

12

post-modern persona of the seventeen year-old poet. The *word* is not the central issue in a poem. Advancing the feeling through the imagery is more important. "Car" speaks to our contemporary American ear & evokes something closer to the voice of the genuine Rimbaud than a perhaps more literal, but historically & emotionally archaic image such as "carriage."

Scholar Wallace Fowlie thinks that *Memory* is Rimbaud's finest poem. The imagery & tone of the final movement of *The Drunken Boat* evokes a similar tone, but is more dynamic. The emotional resolution of *The Drunken Boat* is greater. The theme of *Memory* is only one of the themes of *The Drunken Boat*. The tone of *Memory* is almost elegiac, whereas *The Drunken Boat* stirs the reader's universal longing for freedom. *Memory* is a beautiful poem, but I believe that *The Drunken Boat* is his great masterpiece.

I have included the poem entitled *Eternity* (originally part three of *Festivals Of Patience*, written in 1872) in this edition for several reasons, not least of them that it demonstrates that & how Rimbaud revised his work. *Eternity* first appeared in 1872. The version included here was revised & included in *A Season In Hell* (1873). If he truly intended to leave poetry, why would he revise some of the earlier poems that he incorporated into *A Season In Hell*? Also, remember that scholars are now certain that the *Illuminations* were written in the two years that followed the publication of *A*

Season In Hell. Perhaps expecting consistency from an adolescent boy is the problem here. It is apparent that Rimbaud was often impulsive & fickle in his decisions. His impatience was his Achilles heel.

When one fits *A Season In Hell* into the proper historical context, it becomes an expression of his frustration that he wasn't able to sweep the Parisian literary world off its feet by sheer force & talent. Again, one recognizes his intensity & predominant adolescent impatience.

Ironically, Rimbaud's lined poetry is easier to translate than his prose poems. *Beautiful Being* took me three weeks of hard work to get right. I don't know if I'll ever be able to do justice to *Genie*. The three new ones done for this edition (*Vigils, War* & *One Reason*) illustrate that the *Illuminations* shift between different poetic spaces & levels of abstraction.

The *Illuminations* are Rimbaud at his most experimental. The prose poem form was influenced by Baudelaire, whom Rimbaud, in an early letter, called "A God!" The surfaces are decorative & often overwhelm or take precedence over the thematic content. The imagery is vivid & strung together in imagery-chains & clusters. As in *The Drunken Boat*, the metaphors evolve into symbols. The syntax is complex but ultimately linear, though at points it appears initially to be non-linear.

In the *Illuminations*, Rimbaud invented surrealism. Yet, for all their complexity, *Dawn*, one of the most successful of the prose poems is a simple, straightforward extended metaphor. It also has one of the best first lines in literature: *"I have embraced the summer's dawn."*

His earliest poems reveal a tendency to 'break the rules.' Three of his "I do this, I do that" poems - essentially journal entries - were put into the classic form of the French sonnet. (*Bohemian Life, At The Green Inn & The Clever Maid.*)

I am pleased to finally present these versions in a bi-lingual edition. By comparing my versions to the original French, one may see my rationale for choosing the synonyms I did.

I have generally tried to retain the punctuation & syntax of the originals. Other translators have consistently & unnecessarily altered Rimbaud's punctuation.

These translations were first published in an edition of 500 copies, in 1975, by Free Books Inc. It contained fourteen poems, including *Memory, Marine, The Star, The Wolf, Bohemian Life, Humanity, The Closet, A Winter Dream, Opening Night, The Sleeper In The Valley, Grooves, The Bridges, Phrases* & *The Drunken Boat.*

Most of the copies were given away in Ann Arbor, Michigan, during the annual Ann Arbor Street Fair. David Cope reprinted *The Bridges* in his magazine *Big Scream* in 1976. For the second edition, published by Free Books in 1976, five new translations were added: *O Seasons, O Castles, Ophelia, Shame, Mystic* & *Dawn.* I also added excerpts from two letters by Rimbaud that illustrate

15

his poetic stance as well as his journey from effusive confidence & enthusiasm to despair in a short two year period. For this edition I compared my versions to those of Varese & the translations by Wallace Fowlie.

Poetic translation was seen as a radical liberty in the mid-seventies. In 1971, my college brought Jerome Rothenburg in for a week of lectures, readings & workshops. He had just published *Shaking The Pumpkin*, an anthology of American Indian poetry translated by Rothenburg & other contemporary poets into a vernacular American language, using post-modern structures, breath units & other values of the objectivist movement.

I also met Robert Bly in 1971 under similar circumstances. Robert had begun to do poetic translations himself by then, & one of his talks had focused on the value of translating images, de-emphasizing the exact literal words somewhat by comparison. So, I had an early grounding in the concept of poetic, as opposed to strictly literal translation. We mitigated the debate by referring to our translations as 'versions.'

When these translations were published in 1975, I sent a copy to Bly. Robert wrote that he considered them to be superior to the Varese versions & encouraged me to do more.

The second edition drew brief reviews from the *Small Press Review, Margins* & *Aspects*, a Boston-based magazine edited by the late Ed Hogan. Hogan said *"Greinke's renderings come across with such a remarkably contemporary feel, that he easily gets away with the occasional use of words like 'car' and 'suburbia'. This little collection boasts many fine poems.* The Drunken Boat *is wild and lovely and perhaps the poet's most vivid expression of his desire to find a life of total freedom."*

During the next thirty years, Bly & other poets labored to translate international poets into poetic versions in the contemporary American vernacular. The original 1000 copies of the first editions of my own contribution became valuable collector's items. When I learned of the situation, I began to work on a new edition. *The Drunken Boat* itself is available now as a free world-wide download on my website, www.ericgreinke.com. The greatest anthem to freedom should always be free.

I translated eight new poems for the third edition, published by Presa Press in 2005. (*Fawn's Head, Sensation, My Stolen Heart, Flowers, Royalty, Bottom, Beautiful Being* & *Leaving*.) I sent a copy of the third edition to Bly, who wrote "I still find them wonderful." It's very satisfying to have pleased my old teacher. (He isn't always pleased with me, but that's another story.)

After publication of the third edition, I was also pleased to once again receive support from David Cope, who published *The Drunken Boat* in 2006 for the first time with the French alongside, in his magazine *Big Scream*, thirty years after he'd published *The Bridges* in the same magazine. He has also included *The Drunken Boat* in his new textbook.

Critical response to the third edition has been overwhelmingly positive. Writing in the *Small Press Review* in an article entitled *Rimbaud Alive*, Harry Smith compared my versions to those of Louise Varese & also Paul Schmidt (*Rimbaud: Complete Works*, Harper-Collins). He wrote: *"The latter is less awkward than the former but much more prosaic than Greinke. For music, for the flow, the force of the spirit, Greinke is the easy winner. Although the auditory music of Rimbaud is impossible to capture in English, Greinke is true to the inner music, while giving a sense of the flow of the original. His language is sensuous and wild and feels right."*

It is my hope that this long-awaited bi-lingual edition will find an audience beyond the small press literary world, with students of literature. Rimbaud's vision of the future of poetry & its value as a pathway to increased consciousness was prophetic & right. His own impatience led him on to seek a life of action, but his writing had an energy that lived beyond its creator's neglect. He opened wide the portal of the future, then walked away. Fortunately, he left his keys behind.

-Eric Greinke
1/3/07

The Drunken Boat

Le Bateau ivre

Comme je descendais des Fleuves impassibles,
Je ne me sentis plus guidé par les haleurs:
Des Peaux-Rouges criards les avaient pris pour cibles,
Les ayant cloués nus aux poteaux de couleurs.

J'étais insoucieux de tous les équipages,
Porteur de blés flamands ou de cotons anglais.
Quand avec mes haleurs ont fini ces tapages,
Les Fleuves m'ont laissé descendre où je voulais.

Dans les clapotements furieux des marées,
Moi l'autre hiver, plus sourd que les cerveaux d'enfants,
Je courus! Et les Péninsules démarrées
N'ont pas subi tohu-bohus plus triomphants.

La tempête a béni mes éveils maritimes.
Plus léger qu'un bouchon j'ai dansé sur les flots
Qu'on appelle rouleurs éternels de victimes,
Dix nuits, sans regretter l'œil niais des falots!

Plus douce qu'aux enfants la chair des pommes sures,
L'eau verte pénétra ma coque de sapin
Et des taches de vins bleus et des vomissures
Me lava, dispersant gouvernail et grappin.

Et dès lors, je me suis baigné dans le Poème
De la Mer, infusé d'astres, et lactescent,
Dévorant les azurs verts; où, flottaison blême
Et ravie, un noyé pensif parfois descend;

The Drunken Boat

As I flew down the raving river,
Free at last of the boatman's hands
That nailed themselves to my mast,
That forced me into Indian waters,

I did not miss the stinking crew -
Those pawns of English grain & cotton -
They ran along behind me now,
& the river let me freely flow.

In the roar & whipping of the tide,
I, through that snow, like a child's mind
Rode! & free floating driftwood
Has not known the triumph I have known.

Tempests blessed my mornings on the sea;
I danced on waves as light as foam;
Giant rollers flashed eternal souls,
& at night, I did not miss the lantern's eyes.

As sour apples are sweet to boys,
The green sea penetrated all my seams,
& wine & vomit washed away,
Along with tiller & chains.

Since then I've been bathing in the poem
Of the star-encrusted milky sea,
Drinking in the azure greens, where, pale
& dreaming, a pensive corpse sometimes drifts by;

Où, teignant tout à coup les bleuités, délires
Et rythmes lents sous les rutilements du jour,
Plus fortes que l'alcool, plus vastes que nos lyres,
Fermentent les rousseurs amères de l'amour!

Je sais les cieux crevant en éclairs, et les trombes
Et les ressacs et les courants: je sais le soir,
L'aube exaltée ainsi qu'un peuple de colombes,
Et j'ai vu quelque fois ce que l'homme a cru voir!

J'ai vu le soleil bas, taché d'horreurs mystiques,
Illuminant de longs figements violets,
Pareils à des acteurs de drames très-antiques
Les flots roulant au loin leurs frissons de volets!

J'ai rêvé la nuit verte aux neiges éblouies,
Baiser montant aux yeux des mers avec lenteurs,
La circulation des sèves inouïes,
Et l'éveil jaune et bleu des phosphores chanteurs!

J'ai suivi, des mois pleins, pareille aux vacheries
Hystériques, la houle à l'assaut des récifs,
Sans songer que les pieds lumineux des Maries
Pussent forcer le mufle aux Océans poussifs!

J'ai heurté, savez-vous, d'incroyables Florides
Mêlant aux fleurs des yeux de panthères à peaux
D'hommes! Des arcs-en-ciel tendus comme des brides
Sous l'horizon des mers, à de glauques troupeaux!

J'ai vu fermenter les marais énormes, nasses
Où pourrit dans les joncs tout un Léviathan!
Des écroulement d'eaux au milieu des bonaces,
Et les lointains vers les gouffres cataractant!

& where, abruptly blue, delirious & languid
In the burning day, the rhythms of the sun,
Stronger than alcohol, more vast than song,
Churn in the beaming reds of love!

I've known the skies of light, & waterspouts & waves;
I've known the dark before the rising wings of day;
& sometimes in the twilight I have seen
What other men have only dreamed they've seen!

I've seen the sun descend, strange with mystic signs,
Flashing violet arms like an actor
In an antique tragedy,
Tonal waters escaping in simmering mists.

I've seen green nights & frozen scenes,
Kisses melted on the eyelids of the sea,
Ancient memories bleeding in a stream
Of golden mornings & blue, florescent songs!

I've endured for years the beating surfs,
Mad as crazy cattle leaping for the reefs;
I do not think that Mary's luminous feet
Could still the muzzle of the growling sea!

I've fondled lovely peninsulas,
Mixing flowers with human skin & panther eyes!
Rainbows stretched like endless bridal chains
Beneath the surface of the crowded waves.

I've seen enormous nets, & marshes
Where giants rot amid the reeds;
The sudden splash of white-caps in a calm,
& towering canyons of distant mist.

Glaciers, soleils d'argent, flots nacreux, cieux de braises!
Échouages hideux au fond des golfes bruns
Où les serpents géants dévorés de punaises
Choient, des arbres tordus, avec de noirs parfums!

J'aurais voulu montrer aux enfants ces dorades
Du flot bleu, ces poissons d'or, ces poissons chantants.
- Des écumes de fleurs ont bercé mes dérades
Et d'ineffables vents m'ont ailé par instants.

Parfois, martyr lassé des pôles et des zones,
La mer dont le sanglot faisait mon roulis doux
Montait vers moi ses fleurs d'ombres aux ventouses jaunes
Et je restais, ainsi qu'une femme à genoux...

Presque île, ballottant sur mes bords les querelles
Et les fientes d'oiseaux clabaudeurs aux yeux blonds.
Et je voguais, lorsqu'à travers mes liens frêles
Des noyés descendaient dormir, à reculons!

Or moi, bateau perdu sous les cheveux des anses,
Jeté par l'ouragan dans l'éther sans oiseau,
Moi dont les Monitors et les voiliers des Hanses
N'auraient pas repêché la carcasse ivre d'eau;

Libre, fumant, monté de brumes violettes,
Moi qui trouais le ciel rougeoyant comme un mur
Qui porte, confiture exquise aux bons poëtes,
Des lichens de soleil et des morves d'azur,

Qui courais, taché de lunules électriques,
Planche folle, escorté des hippocampes noirs,
Quand les juillets faisaient crouler à coups de triques
Les cieux ultramarins aux ardents entonnoirs;

Glaciers, silver suns, flaming skies, pearl depths!
Hideous wrecks beneath dusty gulfs,
Where a giant parasitic serpent falls
From a twisted tree, reeking black perfume!

I'll reveal these visions to the children!
These blue surfaces, golden fishes, singing fishes!
The flowering foam has blessed my ride,
& dauntless winds have let me fly!

Sometimes, martyred & weary of zones,
The sea would roll me on her gentle breasts,
& lift me to her shadowed, yellow knees,
& I would sleep upon her lap, then, womanly.

I've sailed the isles, my decks awash
With blood & waste of pale-eyed gulls,
& drifting past my fragile eyes
The sleeping moonbeams fell behind.

I've floated lost amid the cove's hair,
Thrown aloft by storms to where
There are no birds; I could not save the battleships,
My body drunk & bloated there.

Freely fuming, mounted by a purple mist,
I've pierced the deep red wall of clouds
With imagery, my poet's runes:
The lichens of the sun & azure tongues.

Spotted with electric crescent moons,
I've danced along a maddened plank,
As spiral hammers clanged against
The slowly burning, sea-blue heavens.

Moi qui tremblais, sentant geindre à cinquante lieues
Le rut des Béhémots et les Maelstroms épais,
Fileur éternel des immobilités bleues,
Je regrette l'Europe aux anciens parapets!

J'ai vu des archipels sidéraux! et des îles
Dont les cieux délirants sont ouverts au vogueur:
- Est-ce en ces nuits sans fond que tu dors et t'exiles,
Million d'oiseaux d'or, ô future Vigueur? -

Mais, vrai, j'ai trop pleuré! Les Aubes sont navrantes.
Toute lune est atroce et tout soleil amer:
L'âcre amour m'a gonflé de torpeurs enivrantes.
Ô que ma quille éclate! Ô que j'aille à la mer!

Si je désire une eau d'Europe, c'est la flache
Noire et froide où vers le crépuscule embaumé
Un enfant accroupi plein de tristesses, lâche
Un bateau frêle comme un papillon de mai.

Je ne puis plus, baigné de vos langueurs, ô lames,
Enlever leur sillage aux porteurs de cotons,
Ni traverser l'orgueil des drapeaux et des flammes,
Ni nager sous les yeux horribles des pontons.

I've trembled, felt Behemoth's spine,
& heard the groaning of the storms;
I've seen the ancient horror films,
& wished for safe, European walls!

I've seen the islands in space! Islands
Opening windows for the wanderer;
Do you sleep in a night so exiled & deep,
Infinite golden bird, my future Lord?

It's true, I weep too much! Dawn breaks my heart!
Moons are cruel & suns are bitter,
When you have been drunk with love's sad water.
O, let my keel break! O, let me bleed into the sea!

If ever I shall return, it will be to the pond,
Where once, cold & black, toward perfumed evening,
A child on his knees set sail
A leaf as frail as a May butterfly.

I cannot, bathed in your languors, O waves,
Follow the cotton carrier's wake,
Nor salute the bridges of pride & flags,
Nor pass the prison's hulking, horrid shape!

Bonheur

O saisons, ô châteaux,
Quelle âme est sans défaut?

O saisons, ô châteaux,

J'ai fait la magique étude
Du Bonheur, que nul n'élude.

O vive lui, chaque fois
Que chante son coq gaulois.

Mais je n'aurais plus d'envie,
Il s'est chargé de ma vie.

Ce charme ! il prit âme et corps,
Et dispersa tous efforts.

Que comprendre à ma parole?
Il fait qu'elle fuit et vole!

O saisons, ô châteaux!

O Seasons, O Castles

O seasons, O castles,
What soul eludes its fate?

I've made a magic love
Of joy, which no one can escape.

May it live forever, long
As morning birds still sing.

But for me, it's gone away. It
Kidnapped my life, then held

My body hostage. It drained out
My soul, so that now

I cannot speak. Words
Fly off in a mad prison break.

O Seasons! O Castles!
How long must I wait?

Mémoire

1

L'eau claire; comme le sel des larmes d'enfance,
L'assaut au soleil des blancheurs des corps de femmes;
la soie, en foule et de lys pur, des oriflammes
sous les murs dont quelque pucelle eut la défense;

l'ébat des anges; - Non... le courant d'or en marche,
meut ses bras, noirs, et lourds et frais surtout, d'herbe. Elle
sombre, ayant le ciel bleu pour ciel-de-lit, appelle
pour rideaux l'ombre de la colline et de l'arche.

2

Eh! l'humide carreau tend ses bouillons limpides!
L'eau meuble d'or pâle et sans fond les couches prêtes.
Les robes vertes et déteintes des fillettes
font les saules, d'où sautent les oiseaux sans brides.

Plus pure qu'un louis, jaune et chaude paupière
le souci d'eau - ta foi conjugale, ô l'Epouse! -
au midi prompt, de son terne miroir, jalouse
au ciel gris de chaleur la Sphère rose et chère.

3

Madame se tient trop debout dans la prairie
prochaine où neigent les fils du travail; l'ombrelle
aux doigts; foulant l'ombelle; trop fière pour elle,
des enfants lisant dans la verdure fleurie

leur livre de maroquin rouge! Hélas, Lui, comme
mille anges blancs qui se séparent sur la route,
s'éloigne par delà la montagne! Elle, toute
froide et noire, court! après le départ de l'homme!

Memory

1.

The sea is clear, like a child's tear;
White skinned women attack the sun;
Silken banners fold, & lilies fly
Beneath the walls where once a virgin cried.

Angels' work - but no - for a yellow current
Descends, black & heavy, & cool as grass. & she,
Somber, under the sky's blue roof, demands
For her curtains shadows of the hills & arches.

2.

Ah! The limpid surface swirls its dear broth!
Water drowns our fresh-made beds with pale gold!
The soft green robes of the women
Release a swarm of doves from their branches.

Purer than pure gold, a warm & yellow eyelid,
A marshland flower - token of faith, my love -
Promptly at noon, from the murky mirror, duels
The sweet rose Sphere hot in the pale sky.

3.

My lady stands at attention in the field
Where seeds rain down; the umbrella
She holds, & crushes the white petals,
Too proud, in the grass, where a child reads

A red leather book. Sadly, he, as
A thousand white angels choose up sides,
Takes the road beyond the mountain! & she,
All frozen & black, runs after the escaping man!

4
Regrets des bras épais et jeunes d'herbe pure!
Or des lunes d'avril au cœur du saint lit! Joie
des chantiers riverains à l'abandon, en proie
aux soirs d'août qui faisaient germer ces pourritures!

Qu'elle pleure à présent sous les remparts! l'haleine
des peupliers d'en haut est pour la seule brise.
Puis, c'est la nappe, sans reflets, sans source, grise:
un vieux, dragueur, dans sa barque immobile, peine.

5
Jouet de cet œil d'eau morne, je n'y puis prendre,
ô canot immobile! oh! bras trop courts! ni l'une
ni l'autre fleur; ni la jaune qui m'importune,
là; ni la bleue, amie à l'eau couleur de cendre.

Ah! la poudre des saules qu'une aile secoue!
Les roses des roseaux dès longtemps dévorées!
Mon canot toujours fixe; et sa chaîne tirée
Au fond de cet œil d'eau sans bords, - à quelle boue?

4.
I long for the strong young arms of grass!
The golden moons of April in the bed's holy heart;
The joy of abandoned shipyards, victims
To August nights that fertilize the soil!

She is crying now beneath the walls! The breathing
Of the poplar trees is the only breeze. & then,
There is this dull grey surface, without source,
That dredges on, & drives an unmoving boat.

5.
Toy of this sad water's eyes, I am caught,
O unmoving boat! O! Arms are short!   Neither this,
Nor the other flower: not the teasing yellow one,
Nor the comforting blue one in the grey depths!

Ah! The pollen of the willows released by a wing!
The roses of the reeds have been eaten long ago!
My boat, unmoving yet, with its chain tangled
Beneath this shoreless water's eyes, - in what mud?

Marine

Les chars d'argent et de cuivre -
Les proues d'acier et d'argent -
Battent l'écume, -
Soulèvent les souches des ronces.

Les courants de la lande,
Et les ornières immenses du reflux,
Filent circulairement vers l'est,
Vers les piliers de la forêt,
Vers les fûts de la jetée,
Dont l'angle est heurté par des tourbillons de lumière.

Marine

Silver cars with copper trim,
Silver ships with steel trim,
Stir the foam,
& shake the tree-stumps & the thickets.

The currents of the land,
The giant trenches of the tide,
Flow in a circle in the east,
After the columns of the forest,
After the ramparts of the whirlpool,
Against the edges of tornadoes, crashing light.

L'Etoile

L'étoile a pleuré rose au cœur de tes oreilles,
L'infini roulé blanc de ta nuque à tes reins.

La mer a perlé rousse à tes mammes vermeilles,
Et l'Homme saigné noir à ton flanc souverain.

The Star

The star cried like a rose in your listening heart,
& white infinity dripped from your neck to your hips.

The sea turned to rust on your bright red breasts,
& mankind drained black blood on your omnipotent thighs.

Le Loup

Le loup criait sous les feuilles
En crachant les belles plumes
De son repas de volailles:
Comme lui je me consume.

Les salades, les fruits
N'attendent que la cueillette;
Mais l'araignée de la haie
Ne mange que des violettes.

Que je dorme! que je bouille
Aux autels de Salomon.
Le bouillon court sur la rouille,
Et se mêle au Cédron.

The Wolf

The wolf screams beneath the leaves
& scatters the beautiful feathers
Of his dinner in the wind:
I too have eaten my own limbs.

A salad or a bowl of fruit,
Are waiting to be picked,
But the agent in the spider's web
Will only chew a flower.

I want to sleep! I want to boil
On a rich man's stove!
My juices overflow this kettle,
& mingle with the fire below!

Ma Bohème

Je m'en allais, les poings dans mes poches crevées;
Mon paletot aussi devenait idéal;
J'allais sous le ciel, Muse! et j'étais ton féal;
Oh! là là! que d'amours splendides j'ai rêvées!

Mon unique culotte avait un large trou.
- Petit-Poucet rêveur, j'égrenais dans ma course
Des rimes. Mon auberge était à la Grande Ourse.
- Mes étoiles au ciel avaient un doux frou-frou

Et je les écoutais, assis au bord des routes,
Ces bons soirs de septembre où je sentais des gouttes
De rosée à mon front, comme un vin de vigueur;

Où, rimant au milieu des ombres fantastiques,
Comme des lyres, je tirais les élastiques
De mes souliers blessés, un pied près de mon cœur!

Bohemian Life

So I'm walking along, hands in torn-out pockets,
& my coat is really looking perfect
Under the Romantic sky, & I'm a slave
To my dreams of splendid love!

My only pair of pants had a huge hole.
But, as if I was in some fairy tale, I shouted poems
As I went. & I had a room at the Milky Way.
& of course the stars were rustling like leaves.

So, I listened to them, there by the highway underpass,
On those sweet September nights when the rain
& the dew made me drunk as any wine;

& there, rhyming for the fantastic shadows,
& strumming the fibers of my wounded shoes,
I sat: one foot poised above my heart.

Au Cabaret-Vert

Depuis huit jours, j'avais déchiré mes bottines
Aux cailloux des chemins. J'entrais à Charleroi.
- Au Cabaret-Vert: je demandai des tartines
Du beurre et du jambon qui fût à moitié froid.

Bienheureux, j'allongeai les jambes sous la table
Verte: je contemplai les sujets très naïfs
De la tapisserie. - Et ce fut adorable,
Quand la fille aux tétons énormes, aux yeux vifs,

- Celle-là, ce n'est pas un baiser qui l'épeure! -
Rieuse, m'apporta des tartines de beurre,
Du jambon tiède, dans un plat colorié,

Du jambon rose et blanc parfumé d'une gousse
D'ail, - et m'emplit la chope immense, avec sa mousse
Que dorait un rayon de soleil arriéré.

At The Green Inn

For about a week, the soles of my boots
Were torn by the stony roads. I entered Charleroi.
-At the Green Inn: I ordered some bread
With butter & lukewarm ham.

Satisfied, I stretched my legs beneath the table
Of green: I contemplated the simple images
On the wallpaper. - & they were adorable -
When a girl with enormous breasts, & lively eyes,

-That one, never one to avoid embraces! -
Giggling, served me buttered bread,
With warm ham, on a multicolored plate,

With marbled pink ham & flavored by a clove
Of garlic, - & she filled my big mug, with a foamy head
That turned to gold in a ray of sunshine.

La Maline

Dans la salle à manger brune, que parfumait
Une odeur de vernis et de fruits, à mon aise
Je ramassais un plat de je ne sais quel mets
Belge, et je m'épatais dans mon immense chaise.

En mangeant, j'écoutais l'horloge, - heureux et coi.
La cuisine s'ouvrit avec une bouffée,
- Et la servante vint, je ne sais pas pourquoi,
Fichu moitié défait, malinement coiffée

Et, tout en promenant son petit doigt tremblant
Sur sa joue, un velours de pêche rose et blanc,
En faisant, de sa lèvre enfantine, une moue,

Elle arrangeait les plats, près de moi, pour m'aiser;
- Puis, comme ça, - bien sûr pour avoir un baiser, -
Tout bas: "Sens donc: j'ai pris une froid sur la joue..."

The Clever Maid

In the brown dinette, perfumed
With the aroma of varnish & of fruits, at my ease
I scarfed a plate of various foreign
Delicacies, & I sprawled in my big chair.

As I ate, I heard the clock, in joyful silence.
The kitchen door burst open,
-& a serving maid entered, I knew not why,
Her throat exposed, her hair cleverly mussed.

&, as she trembled her little finger
Across her cheek, of peachy pink & white skin,
Pouting, like a child, with her lips,

She rearranged the plates, coming casually close;
-Then, just so - subtly, to sneak a kiss, -
Said softly: "Feel here: I've caught a cold on my cheek..."

L'Humanité Chaussait

L'Humaniaté chaussait le vaste enfant Progrès.

Humanity

Humanity was putting shoes on the vast child Progress.

Le Buffet

C'est un large buffet sculpté; le chêne sombre,
Très vieux, a pris cet air si bon des vieilles gens;
Le buffet est ouvert, et verse dans son ombre
Comme un flot de vin vieux, des parfums engageants;

Tout plein, c'est un fouillis de vieilles vieilleries,
De linges odorants et jaunes, de chiffons
De femmes ou d'enfants, de dentelles flétries,
De fichus de grand'mère où sont peints des griffons;

- C'est là qu'on trouverait les médaillons, les mèches
De cheveux blancs ou blonds, les portraits, les fleurs sèches
Dont le parfum se mêle à des parfums de fruits.

- O buffet du vieux temps, tu sais bien des histoires,
Et tu voudrais conter tes contes, et tu bruis
Quand s'ouvrent lentement tes grandes portes noires.

The Closet

It is a large carved closet made of
Old dark oak, & it has the quality of
An old person. The door is open, & a shadow
Of an odor descends your throat like vintage wine.

It is full of strange antiques:
Of yellow sheets, old clothing,
Of women & children, of faded lace,
Of ancient cloaks embroidered with ghosts.

You could find medals, locks
Of blonde hair, tiny portraits, dried flowers
Mingling with the smell of fruit.

My closet, you know what has happened,
& you would tell me, & I can hear you whispering
When you slowly open your big black doors.

Rêvé Pour L'hiver

L'hiver, nous irons dans un petit wagon rose
Avec des coussins bleus.
Nous serons bien. Un nid de baisers fous repose
Dans chaque coin moelleux.

Tu fermeras l'œil, pour ne point voir, par la glace,
Grimacer les ombres des soirs,
Ces monstruosités hargneuses, populace
De démons noirs et de loups noirs.

Puis tu te sentiras la joue égratignée...
Un petit baiser, comme une folle araignée,
Te courra par le cou...

Et tu me diras : "Cherche!", en inclinant la tête,
- Et nous prendrons du temps à trouver cette bête
- Qui voyage beaucoup...

A Winter Dream

This winter, we'll depart in a little pink car
With a blue interior.
We will be satisfied. Baskets of kisses are waiting
In soft, upholstered corners.

When the evening shadows make ugly faces in the glass,
You will close your eyes,
So as not to see the snarling monsters, & the cities
Of black demons & wolves.

& then you will feel a little scratch on the cheek -
Just a little kiss, running like a crazed spider
Around your white neck -

& you will say to me: "Get it off!"-
& I will search for it for a very long time.
Because those little spiders can really move.

Ophélie

I

Sur l'onde calme et noire où dorment les étoiles
La blanche Ophélia flotte comme un grand lys,
Flotte très lentement, couchée en ses longs voiles...
- On entend dans les bois lointains des hallalis.

Voici plus de mille ans que la triste Ophélie
Passe, fantôme blanc, sur le long fleuve noir.
Voici plus de mille ans que sa douce folie
Murmure sa romance à la brise du soir.

Le vent baise ses seins et déploie en corolle
Ses grands voiles bercés mollement par les eaux;
Les saules frissonnants pleurent sur son épaule,
Sur son grand front rêveur s'inclinent les roseaux.

Les nénuphars froissés soupirent autour d'elle;
Elle éveille parfois, dans un aune qui dort,
Quelque nid, d'où s'échappe un petit frisson d'aile:
- Un chant mystérieux tombe des astres d'or

II

O pâle Ophélia! belle comme la neige!
Oui tu mourus, enfant, par un fleuve emporté!
C'est que les vents tombant des grand monts de Norwège
T'avaient parlé tout bas de l'âpre liberté;

C'est qu'un souffle, tordant ta grande chevelure,
A ton esprit rêveur portait d'étranges bruits,
Que ton cœur écoutait le chant de la Nature
Dans les plaintes de l'arbre et les soupirs des nuits;

Ophelia

1.
On the black dead water where stars still sleep,
A great white lily, Ophelia, floats;
Her long sheets of hair float about her skull.
You hear on shore the sound of the kill.

Sad Ophelia, always passing,
Pale & white, down the long black stream.
One thousand years & still sweet madness
Whispers her name in the wind.

Her breasts are kissed by the wind.
Her veil is wreathed by the sea.
Tender willows sway & cry, & reeds
Bend low to touch her dreaming eyes.

Tired lilies sigh around, & often,
She wakes, in wet nightgown,
In a foreign nest, as wings escape.
Mysterious singing sprinkles from the golden stars.

2.
Ophelia: pale & beautiful as snow!
You died, sweet child, mated to a river!
Bitter winds fell off a mountain
To harshly speak of freedom.

A great breath twisted your hair
With strange rumors, in a dream.
Your heart listened to the Universal Song
In the creaking trees & the breathing night.

C'est que la voix des mers folles, immense râle,
Brisait ton sein d'enfant, trop humain et trop doux;
C'est qu'un matin d'avril, un beau cavalier pâle,
Un pauvre fou, s'assit muet à tes genoux!

Ciel! Amour! Liberté! Quel rêve, ô pauvre Folle!
Tu te fondais à lui comme une neige au feu;
Tes grandes visions étranglaient ta parole
- Et l'Infini terrible éffara ton œil bleu!

III
- Et le Poète dit qu'aux rayons des étoiles
Tu viens chercher, la nuit, les fleurs que tu cueillis;
Et qu'il a vu sur l'eau, couchée en ses longs voiles,
La blanche Ophélia flotter, comme un grand lys.

The booming voice of the loony sea
Broke your new heart, too human & soft.
A mad pale knight sat mute
At your knees, on that April day.

Heaven! Love! Freedom! What dreams, O mad girl!
You melted on him like snow in a fire!
Your visions stumbled among your words,
& cold infinity exploded in your blue eyes!

3.
Under the rays of the stony stars
I went for the flowers I left;
& on the black waves, all veiled in white,
A giant white lily, Ophelia, slept.

Honte

Tant que la lame n'aura
Pas coupé cette cervelle,
Ce paquet blanc, vert et gras,
A vapeur jamais nouvelle,

(Ah! Lui, devrait couper son
Nez, sa lèvre, ses oreilles,
Son ventre! et faire abandon
De ses jambes! ô merveille!)

Mais non, vrai, je crois que tant
Que pour sa tête la lame,
Que les cailloux pour son flanc,
Que pour ses boyaux la flamme

N'auront pas agi, l'enfant
Gêneur, la si sotte bête,
Ne doit cesser un instant
De ruser et d'être traître.

Comme un chat des Monts-Rocheux,
D'empuantir toutes sphères!
Qu'à sa mort pourtant, ô mon Dieu!
S'élève quelque prière!

Shame

For now, no razorblade
Has cut out his brain,
That green mass of fat,
& ancient steam.

(Hah! He should cut off his
Nose, his lips, his ears, spill
His guts & abandon
His legs! A favor!)

Not really. No, I believe
That as long as the blade on his head,
The boulder on his ribs,
The bonfire on his breast

Holds off, the idiot child,
Annoying & dull as a bull,
Should never give up
His cheating heart.

He's an evil killer cat,
Stenching up the world.
But, as he dies, O God,
Let his voice be heard.

Première Soirée

Elle était fort déshabillée
Et de grands arbres indiscrets
Aux vitres jetaient leur feuillée
Malinement, tout près, tout près.

Assise sur ma grande chaise,
Mi-nue, elle joignait les mains.
Sur le plancher frissonnaient d'aise
Ses petits pieds si fins, si fins

Je regardai, couleur de cire
Un petit rayon buissonnier
Papillonner dans son sourire
Et sur son sein, - mouche ou rosier.

Je baisai ses fines chevilles.
Elle eut un doux rire brutal
Qui s'égrenait en claires trilles,
Un joli rire de cristal.

Les petits pieds sous la chemise
Se sauvèrent: "Veux-tu en finir!"
La première audace permise,
Le rire feignait de punir!

Pauvrets palpitants sous ma lèvre,
Je baisai doucement ses yeux:
Elle jeta sa tête mièvre
En arrière : "Oh! c'est encor mieux!...

Opening Night

She was almost nude
& big bold trees
Threw their leaves against the glass
So cleverly: pressing, pressing.

Sitting in my chair,
Her hands were tightly closed.
Alive with joy on the floor,
Her tiny feet were frail, so frail.

Pale, I watched
A nervous strand of light
Flicker on her lips,
& on her breast, the tattoo of a rose.

I kissed her fragile knees.
She laughed quickly, the soft sound
Spreading in a clear thrilling arc,
The sound ringing like crystal.

The little feet beneath the nightgown
Pulled up. "Please stop!"
-When the first attempt succeeded,
The laughter pretended to scold!

Pitiful & trembling under my lips,
I gently kissed her eyes:
-She threw back her head:
"Oh! It's more than I can stand!"

"Monsieur, j'ai deux mots à te dire..."
Je lui jetai le reste au sein
Dans un baiser, qui la fit rire
D'un bon rire qui voulait bien.....

Elle était fort déshabillée
Et de grands arbres indiscrets
Aux vitres jetaient leur feuillée
Malinement, tout près, tout près.

"I have to tell you, Sir..."
I finished on her breast
With a kiss, which she couldn't resist,
& she laughed then, willingly....

She was almost nude
& big bold trees
Threw their leaves against the glass
So cleverly: pressing, pressing.

Le Dormeur du Val

C'est un trou de verdure où chante une rivière
Accrochant follement aux herbes des haillons
D'argent; où le soleil, de la montagne fière,
Luit: c'est un petit val qui mousse de rayons.

Un soldat jeune, lèvre bouche ouverte, tête nue,
Et la nuque baignant dans le frais cresson bleu,
Dort; il est étendu dans l'herbe sous la nue,
Pâle dans son lit vert où la lumière pleut.

Les pieds dans les glaïeuls, il dort. Souriant comme
Sourirait un enfant malade, il fait un somme:
Nature, berce-le chaudement: il a froid.

Les parfums ne font pas frissonner sa narine;
Il dort dans le soleil, la main sur sa poitrine,
Tranquille. Il a deux trous rouges au côté droit.

The Sleeper In The Valley

A river sings in a yellow hollow,
& catches the silver clothing of the grass,
Where the sun reflects the mountain's pride:
A little valley swirling with light.

A teenage soldier, with open mouth & bare head,
With his head awash in the cool blue weeds,
Sleeps; he is prone; on the grass beneath the clouds,
Pale on a green bed, in a luminous rain.

His feet are in the gladiolas. He sleeps. Smiling
As a dying child, he is taking a brief rest:
Nature, rock him in your warm arms: he freezes.

His nostrils will not quiver to the strongest perfume.
He is asleep in the sun, his hands on his breast,
Peacefully. There are two red holes beneath his heart.

Tête de Faune

Dans la feuillée, écrin vert taché d'or,
Dans la feuillée incertaine et fleurie
De fleurs splendides où le baiser dort,
Vif et crevant l'exquise broderie,

Un faune effaré montre ses deux yeux
Et mord les fleurs rouges de ses dents blanches.
Brunie et sanglante ainsi qu'un vin vieux,
Sa lèvre éclate en rires sous les branches.

Et quand il a fui - tel qu'un écureuil -
Son rire tremble encore à chaque feuille,
Et l'on voit épeuré par un bouvreuil
Le Baiser d'or du Bois, qui se recueille.

Fawn's Head

In the forest, green-gold jewelry-box,
In the forest, half-hidden
By splendid flowers kissed with sleep,
Life breaks through the fine blanket,

A frightened fawn reveals both his eyes
& bites the red flowers with his white teeth.
Brown & bloodstained as ancient wine,
His lips explode with laughter beneath the branches.

& after he's escaped - like a wily squirrel -
His voice trembles within every leaf,
& we spy the fearful bullfinch,
The Golden Kiss of the Woods, as he meditates.

Sensation

Par les soirs bleus d'été, j'irai dans les sentiers,
Picoté par les blés, fouler l'herbe menue:
Rêveur, j'en sentirai la fraîcheur à mes pieds.
Je laisserai le vent baigner ma tête nue.

Je ne parlerai pas, je ne penserai rien:
Mais l'amour infini me montera dans l'âme,
Et j'irai loin, bien loin, comme un bohémien,
Par la nature - heureux comme avec une femme.

Sensation

In summer blue evenings, I'll walk the trails
Picking my way through stubby prickles of grass
In revery, feeling its coolness fresh on my feet.
I'll bathe my naked head in the new wind.

I will not speak, I will not think:
But infinite love will rise in my soul,
& I'll travel, travel far away, like a refugee,
Through the country - thrilled like I'm with a girl.

Le Cœur Volé

Mon triste coeur bave à la poupe,
Mon cœur couvert de caporal:
Ils y lancent des jets de soupe
Mon triste cœur bave à la poupe:
Sous les quolibets de la troupe
Qui pousse un rire général,
Mon triste cœur bave à la poupe,
Mon cœur couvert de caporal!

Ithyphalliques et pioupiesques,
Leurs quolibets l'ont dépravé!
Au gouvernail, on voit des fresques
Ithyphalliques et pioupiesques.
O flots abracadabrantesques,
Prenez mon cœur, qu'il soit lavé!
Ithyphalliques et pioupiesques,
Leurs quolibets l'ont dépravé!

Quand ils auront tari leurs chiques
Comment agir, ô cœur volé?
Ce seront des hoquets bachiques
Quand ils auront tari leurs chiques:
J'aurai des sursauts stomachiques,
Moi, si mon cœur est ravalé:
Quand ils auront tari leurs chiques
Comment agir, ô cœur volé ?

My Stolen Heart

My sad heart gushes in poop,
My heart drenched in tobacco spit:
They vomit currents of soup
My sad heart drowns in shit:
Beneath the ridicule of the troop
Bursting with hilarious taunts,
My sad heart gushes in poop,
My heart drenched in tobacco spit!

Ithyphallic & military,
Their sarcasm has dirtied it!
You see pictures on the tiller.
Ithyphallic & military.
Oh waves of magic,
Seize my heart, & wash it!
Ithyphallic & military,
Their sarcasm has dirtied it.

When all their wages are spent,
How to get you back, oh stolen heart?
There will be burps of wine
When all their wages are spent:
I'll feel my stomach turn,
When my heart has been ravaged:
When all their wages are spent
How to get you back, oh stolen heart?

L'Eternité

Elle est retrouvée!
Quoi? l'éternité.
C'est la mer allée
      Au soleil.

Mon âme éternelle,
Observe ton vœu
Malgré la nuit seule
Et le jour en feu.

Done tu te dégages
Des humains suffrages,
Des communs élans!
Tu voles selon...

-Jamais l'espérance,
Pas d'orietur.
Science et patience,
Le supplice est sûr.

Plus de lendemain,
Braises de satin,
Votre ardeur
Est le devoir.

Elle est retrouvée!
-Quoi? - l'Eternité.
C'est la mer allée
      Au soleil.

Eternity

It is regained!
What? eternity.
In the sea mixed
          With sunshine.

My soul eternal
Observe your vow
Regardless of the night
& the burning day.

For then, you disengage
From human suffering,
From common striving!
You take flight accordingly...

Without hope,
No direction.
Science & patience,
The suffering is assured.

No more tomorrow,
Satin embers,
Your desire
Is devotion.

It is regained!
What? Eternity.
In the sea mixed
          With sunshine.

From The Letters

15May1871

Si le cuivre s'éveille clairon, il n'y a rien de a faute. Cela m'est évident: j'assiste à l'éclosion de ma pensée: je la regarde, je l'écoute: je lance un coup d'archet: la symphonie fair son remuement dans les profondeurs, ou vient d'un bond sur la scène.

****

La première étude de l'homme qui veut être poète est sa propre connaissance, entière; il cherche son âme, il l'inspecte, il la tente, l'apprend. Dès qu'il la sait, il doit la cultiver!

****

Donc le poète est vraiment voleur de feu. Il est chargé de l'humanité, des animaux même.

****

Trouver une langue. -Du reste, toute parole étant idée, le temps d'un langage universel viendra!

****

Cette langue sera de l'âme pour l'âme, résumant tout, parfums, sons, couleurs, de la pensée accrochant la pensée et tirant. Le poête définirait la quantité d'inconnu s'éveillant en son temps dans l'âme universelle: il donnerait plus - que la formule de sa pensée, que l'annotation de sa marche au Progrès! Enormité devenant norme, absorbée par tous, il serait vraiment un multiplicateur de progrès!

From The Letters

15 MAY 1871
If brass wakes up a horn, it's not its fault. It's obvious to me.
I am there as my thoughts are born. I watch them & listen to
them. Now I strike the bow: the symphony stirs in its depths,
or leaps to the stage.

*

The first study of he who wants to be a poet is the complete
knowledge of himself. He searches for his soul, tastes it, tests
it, learns it. As soon as he knows it, he must cultivate it!

*

The poet is truly the thief of fire. He is responsible for
humanity, & for the animals.

*

A language must be found! Every word being an idea, the day
of a Universal Language will come!

*

It will be a language of the soul for the soul, containing
everything: smells, sounds, colors, thoughts holding on to
thoughts & pulling. The poet will define that part of the
unknown awakening in his time in the Universal Soul: he will
give more than the mere formation of his thought, more than
just the notes taken on his personal march toward Progress.
Enormity becoming normal, absorbed by all, he will really BE
PROGRESS, & it will multiply through him!

From The Letters

7May1873
*Maintenant c'est la nuit que je travaince. De minuit à cinq
heures du matin. Le mois passé, ma chambre, ru Monsieur-le-
Prince, donnait sur un jardin du lycée Saint-Louis. Il y avait
des arbres énormes sous ma fenêtre étroite. A trois heures du
matin, la bougie pâlit: tous les oiseaux crient à la fois dans les
arbres: c'est fini. Plus de travail. I! me fallait regarder les
arbres, le ciel, saisis par cette heure indicible, première du
matin. Je voyoais les dortoirs du lycée, absolument sourds.
Et déjà le bruit saccadé, sonore, délicieux des tombereaux sur
les boulevards. - Je fumais ma pipe-marteau, en crachant sur
les tuiles, car c'était une mansarde, ma chambre. A cinq
heures, je descendais à l'achat de quelque pain: c'est l'heure.
Les ouvriers sont en marche partout. C'est l'heure de se soûler
chez les marchands de vin, pour moi. Je rentrais manger, et
me couchais à sept heures du matin, quand le soleil faisait
sortir les cloportes de dessous les tuiles. Le premier matin en
été, et les soirs de décembre, voilà ce qui m'a ravi toujours ici.*

From The Letters

7 MAY 1873
Now I am crossing through the night. Midnight to 5AM. Last
month my room overlooked a garden. There were huge trees
beneath my narrow window. At 3AM, the last candle went out:
all the birds cry out at once in the trees: it's finished. No more
work. Then I had to look at the trees & the sky, seized by that
unspeakable hour, the first morning. I looked across at the
lycee dorms, absolutely muted. Already the chopping, lovely
noise of the carts on the boulevards. I smoked my pipe, & spit
on the tiles. My room was a loft. At 5AM, I went downstairs to
buy bread. It was time. Workmen were walking everywhere,
but for me it was time to get drunk on wine & return to my
room to eat, then fall asleep at 7AM, when the sun brought the
woodlice from under the tiles. An early morning sun in June
still turns me on. And December nights.

Mystique

Sur la pente du talus, les anges tournent leurs robes de laine dans les herbages d'acier et d'émeraude.

Des prés de flammes bondissent jusqu'au sommet du mamelon. À gauche, le terreau de l'arête est piétiné par tous les homicides et toutes les batailles, et tous les bruits désastreux filent leur courbe. Derrière l'arête de droite, la ligne des orients, des progrès.

Et tandis que la bande en haut du tableau est formée de la rumeur tournante et bondissante des conques des mers et des nuits humaines,

La douceur fleurie des étoiles et du ciel et du reste descend en face du talus, comme un panier, - contre notre face, et fait l'abîme fleurant et bleu là-dessous.

Mystic

The angels whirl their woolen skins on the emerald slope of the steel hill.

Flaming fields leap to the crest. On the left, the ridge is scarred by numerous wars & homicides. Catastrophic noise describes its curve. Behind the right hand edge, the line of Oriental Progress forms.

& while the band strikes up above the picture, composed of empty conch-shells & human dreams,

the fragrant stars blossom in the night & the universe descends opposite the hill like a shade pulled down in front of my face & sweet scents rise from the blue canyon below.

Aube

J'ai embrassé l'aube d'été.

Rien ne bougeait encore au front des palais. L'eau était morte. Les camps d'ombres ne quittaient pas la route du bois. J'ai marché, réveillant les haleines vives et tièdes, et les pierreries regardèrent, et les ailes se levèrent sans bruit.

La première entreprise fut, dans le sentier déjà empli de frais et blêmes éclats, une fleur qui me dit son nom.

Je ris au wasserfall blond qui s'échevela à travers les sapins: à la cime argentée je reconnus la déesse.

Alors, je levai un à un les voiles. Dans l'allée, en agitant les bras. Par la plaine, où je l'ai dénoncée au coq. A la grand'ville elle fuyait parmi les clochers et les dômes, et courant comme un mendiant sur les quais de marbre, je la chassais.

En haut de la route, près d'un bois de lauriers, je l'ai entourée avec ses voiles amassées, et j'ai senti un peu son immense corps. L'aube et l'enfant tombèrent au bas du bois.

Au réveil il était midi.

Dawn

I have embraced the summer dawn.

The palace faces slept, & the water was dead. Shadows were painted on the road to the woods, where I walked, waking up the warm, living air. Rocks stared coldly, & wings flew off without a sound.

My first date was on a cool, lighted path, where a flower told me its name.

I laughed at the blonde waterfall splashing in the pines: & then I saw the goddess, standing on the silver peak.

Little by little I peeled off her veil, there, on the path, & I waved my wild arms! & then, on the plain, where I woke up the cock. Then she ran to the City, through steeples & domes, & out among the marble wharves, & I chased her.

As the road rose by a laurel wood, I wrapped her in her frozen veil, feeling the galaxies of her body. Dawn & a child fell by the forest border.

When I awoke, it was already noon.

Veillées

I

C'est le repos éclairé, ni fièvre ni langueur, sur le lit ou sur le pré.

C'est l'ami ni ardent ni faible. L'ami.

C'est l'aimée ni tourmentante ni tourmentée. L'aimée.

L'air et le monde point cherchés. La vie.

– Etait-ce donc ceci ?

– Et le rêve fraîchit.

II

L'éclairage revient à l'arbre de bâtisse. Des deux extrémités de la salle, décors quelconques, des élévations harmoniques se joignent. La muraille en face du veilleur est une succession psychologique de coupes, de frises de bandes atmosphériques et d'accidents géologiques. – Rêve intense et rapide de groupes sentimentaux avec des êtres de tous les caractères parmi toutes les apparences.

III

Les lampes et les tapis de la veillée font le bruit des vagues, la nuit, le long de la coque et autour du steerage.

La mer de la veillée, telle que les seins d'Amélie.

Les tapisseries, jusqu'à mi-hauteur, des taillis de dentelle teinte d'émeraude, où se jettent les tourterelles de la veillée.

. . . .

La plaque du foyer noir, de réels soleils des grèves: ah! puits des magies; seule vue d'aurore, cette fois.

Vigils

1.
It reposes in light, neither fever nor languor, on the bed or on
the meadow.

It is the friend, neither weak nor strong. The friend.

It is the beloved, neither tortuous nor tortured. The beloved.

The air & the world ignored. Life.

- Was this it, then?

- & the dream froze.

2.
The lighting returns to the pillar. From the opposite sides of
the room, of questionable decor, harmonies rise to merge. The
wall that faces the viewer is a series of mental images of friezes,
atmospheric orchestras & geological accidents. - An intense
short dream of sentimental groups of divergent characters in
every possible appearance.

3.
The lamps & the carpets of the vigil make the sound of waves,
at night, slapping along the hull & around the prop.

The sea of the vigil, like the breasts of Emily.

The tapestries, halfway up the wall, the thatch of lace tinted
emerald, where the doves of the vigil fly.

. . . .

The plague of dark earth, the real sun of the shores. ah!
wells of magic; the only dawn in sight, for now.

Ornières

A droite l'aube d'été éveille les feuilles et les vapeurs et les bruits de ce coin du parc, et les talus de gauche tiennent dans leur ombre violette les mille rapides ornières de la route humide. Défilé de féeries. En effet: des chars chargés d'animaux de bois doré, de mâts et de toiles bariolées, au grand galop de vingt chevaux de cirque tachetés, et les enfants, et les hommes, sur leurs bêtes les plus étonnantes; - vingt véhicules, bossés, pavoisés et fleuris comme des carrosses anciens ou de contes, pleins d'enfants attifés pour une pastorale suburbaine. - même des cercueils sous leur dais de nuit dressant les panaches d'ébène, filant au trot des grandes juments bleues et noires.

Grooves

On your right the summer dawn shakes the leaves awake, & the fog & the traffic in the park, & the banks along the left caress with violet hands of shadow the thousand canyons of the drunken road.

Lines of fairies! Yes! See the floats of giant glided wooden animals, their poles & paper buntings, to the angry gallop of the twenty speckled circus horses, & kids & grownups on their fabulous beasts: - twenty spherical cars, decorated with flowers & flags like oldtime coaches of snappy children, pastoral in suburbia.

Even the coffins beneath the grey tents rise & float among the shiny black feathers, rolling along to the measure of the grandiose horses, blue & black.

Les Ponts

Des ciels gris de cristal. Un bizarre dessin de ponts, ceux-ci droits, ceux-là bombés, d'autres descendant ou obliquant en angles sur les premiers, et ces figures se renouvelant dans les autres circuits éclairés du canal, mais tous tellement longs et légers que les rives, chargées de dômes, s'abaissent et s'amoindrissent. Quelques-uns de ces ponts sont encore chargés de masures. D'autres soutiennent des mâts, des signaux, de frêles parapets. Des accords mineurs se croisent et filent, des cordes montent des berges. On distingue une veste rouge, peut-être d'autres costumes et des instruments de musique. Sont-ce des airs populaires, des bouts de concerts seigneuriaux, des restants d'hymnes publics? L'eau est grise et bleue, large comme un bras de mer.

- Un rayon blanc, tombant du haut du ciel, anéantit cette comédie.

The Bridges

In the crystal grey sky there is a mad arrangement of bridges; some straight, some bending in high arches, others falling at hard angles to the first. These figures dot the lighted paths of the canal, & eventually, with all this wealth, the banks shrink, then sink away.

Traffic lights, stores, street-signs & fragile railings grow from the bridges. Minor chords cross one another, disengage, & disappear. Ropes rise from the shore.

I can distinguish a red coat, & perhaps a clown suit & some musical instruments. Would these be pop songs, pieces of classical symphonies, or the remnants of church-hymns? The water, blue & grey, spreads from the arm of the sea in a varicose vein.

A white ray tumbles above the clouds & brings an abrupt end to this merciless comedy.

Phrases

Quand le monde sera réduit en un seul bois noir pour nos quatre yeux étonnés, - en une plage pour deux enfants fidèles, - en une maison musicale pour notre claire sympathie, - je vous trouverai.

Qu'il n'y ait ici-bas qu'un vieillard seul, calme et beau, entouré d'un "luxe inouï", - et je suis à vos genoux.

Que j'aie réalisé tous vos souvenirs, - que je sois celle qui sait vous garrotter, - je vous étoufferai.

~~~~~~~~~~~~~~~~~~~~~~

Quand nous sommes très forts, - qui recule? très gais, qui tombe de ridicule? Quand nous sommes très méchants, que ferait-on de nous?

Parez-vous, dansez, riez, - Je ne pourrai jamais envoyer l'Amour par la fenêtre.

~~~~~~~~~~~~~~~~~~~~~~

Ma camarade, mendiante, enfant monstre! comme ça t'est égal, ces malheureuses et ces manoeuvres, et mes embarras. Attache-toi à nous avec ta voix impossible, ta voix! unique flatteur de ce vil désespoir.

~~~~~~~~~~~~~~~~~~~~~~

Une matinée couverte, en juillet. Un goût de cendres vole dans l'air; - une odeur de bois suant dans l'âtre, - les fleurs rouies, - le saccage des promenades, - la bruine des canaux par les champs, - pourquoi pas déjà les joujoux et l'encens?

Phrases

When the world is reduced to a black tree for the two of us, sand for our faith, musical walls for our love, I'll find you.

If I look down, & see only an old man, beautiful & relaxed in the midst of incredible luxury, look toward your feet, & I'll be there.

If it turns out that I'm what you remember, or if I turn out to be your conqueror, then I'll strangle you.

* * * * * * * * * * * * * * * * * * *

When you're strong, are you gonna run? When you're happy, do you want to be mocked? When we're really bad, what the hell are they going to do with us?

Get all dressed up! Dance around! Laugh! I never could throw love out the window!

* * * * * * * * * * * * * * * * * * *

My companion, panhandler, infant monster! My embarrassment doesn't mean a thing to you - the sad women & the games - the games! Climb on us with your impossible voice - your voice!- savior from this ugly despair!

* * * * * * * * * * * * * * * * * * *

A dark morning in July. A taste of ashes floats in the air. A smell of damp wood on the fire. Dew wet flowers. Destruction along the bike paths. Fog creeps from the low canal onto the field. What has happened to the incense, & where are my toys?

J'ai tendu des cordes de clocher à clocher; des guirlandes de fenêtre à fenêtre; des chaînes d'or d'étoile à étoile, et je danse.

~~~~~~~~~~~~~~~~~~~~~~~

Le haut étang fume continuellement. Quelle sorcière va se dresser sur le couchant blanc? Quelles violettes frondaisons vont descendre?

~~~~~~~~~~~~~~~~~~~~~~~

Pendant que les fonds publics s'écoulent en fêtes de fraternité, il sonne une cloche de feu rose dans les nuages.

~~~~~~~~~~~~~~~~~~~~~~~

Avivant un agréable goût d'encre de Chine, une poudre noire pleut doucement sur ma veillée. - Je baisse les feux du lustre, je me jette sur le lit, et, tourné du côté de l'ombre, je vous vois, mes filles! mes reines!

I've made bridges of string from one steeple to another, & garlands from one window to another: chains of gold, swinging from star to star, & I can dance.

* * * * * * * * * * * * * * * * * * *

The pond in the hills is always smoking. What magic will lift into the white western sky? & what purple frost will fall?

* * * * * * * * * * * * * * * * * * *

As public funds evaporate in feasts of brotherhood, a bell of rosy flames bellows in the clouds.

* * * * * * * * * * * * * * * * * * *

A pleasant aftertaste of Indian ink, black powder rains on my vigil. I turn down the lamp, throw myself on the bed, & with my face arrested by the shadow, I recognize you: my daughters & my queens!

Fleurs

D'un gradin d'or, - parmi les cordons de soie, les gazes grises, les velours verts et les disques de cristal qui noircissent comme du bronze au soleil, - je vois la digitale s'ouvrir sur un tapis de filigranes d'argent, d'yeux et de chevelures.

Des pièces d'or jaune semées sur l'agate, des piliers d'acajou supportant un dôme d'émeraudes, des bouquets de satin blanc et de fines verges de rubis entourent la rose d'eau.

Tels qu'un dieu aux énormes yeux bleus et aux formes de neige, la mer et le ciel attirent aux terrasses de marbre la foule des jeunes et fortes roses.

Flowers

From a golden balcony amid the ropes of silk, the veils of grey, the green velvets & plates of crystal, dark as sunlit bronze - I see the flowers waking on a tapestry of silver threads, & their eyes & their hair.

Pieces of amber gold planted on the agate pillars of dark wood hold up an emerald dome, the bouquets of white satin & fine stems of rubies encircle the floating roses.

Like a god with enormous eyes of blue & a body of snow, the ocean & the sky lure the throng of strong, young roses up the marble stairway.

Royauté

Un beau matin, chez un peuple fort doux, un homme et une femme superbes criaient sur la place publique: "Mes amis, je veux qu'elle soit reine!" "Je veux être reine!" Elle riait et tremblait. Il parlait aux amis de révélation, d'épreuve terminée. Ils se pâmaient l'un contre l'autre.

En effet ils furent rois toute une matinée où les tentures carminées se relevèrent sur les maisons, et tout l'après-midi, où ils s'avancèrent du côté des jardins de palmes.

Royalty

One fine morning, in a country of soft people, a man & a pretty woman made a public declaration: "My friends, here is your Queen!" "I want to be Queen." She laughed, trembling. He told them of his revelation that their problems would soon be over. They all celebrated & congratulated each other.

In effect, they were monarchs before noon, & purple banners hung from the houses all afternoon as they paraded toward the courtyard of the palms.

Bottom

La réalité étant trop épineuse pour mon grand caractère, - je me trouvai néanmoins chez ma dame, en gros oiseau gris bleu s'essorant vers les moulures du plafond et traînant l'aile dans les ombres de la soirée.

Je fus, au pied du baldaquin supportant ses bijoux adorés et ses chef-d'oeuvre physiques, un gros ours aux gencives violettes et au poil chenu de chagrin, les yeux aux cristaux et aux argents des consoles.

Tout se fit ombre et aquarium ardent.

Au matin - aube de juin batailleuse, - je courus aux champs, âne, claironnant et brandissant mon grief, jusqu'à ce que les Sabines de la banlieue vinrent se jeter à mon poitrail.

Bottom

With reality being too sharp for my grand ego, in my lady's name, a big bird of blue & gray violently dragged my wings to the corners of the ceiling following the evening shadows.

At the foot of the balcony that supported her adorable jewels & physical masterpieces, I became a great gross bear with purple gums & thick, messy fur, with eyes of crystal & silver for consolation.

Night fell dark as an aquarium of fire.

By morning, June dawn battleground - I ran the lawn, an ass, braying & brandishing my grief, until the Sabines arrived from the edge of town to throw themselves over my beastly breast.

Being Beauteous

Devant une neige un Etre de Beauté de haute taille. Des sifflements de mort et des cercles de musique sourde font monter, s'élargir et trembler comme un spectre ce corps adoré; des blessures écarlates et noires éclatent dans les chairs superbes. Les couleurs propres de la vie se foncent, dansent, et se dégagent autour de la Vision, sur le chantier. Et les frissons s'élèvent et grondent et la saveur forcenée de ces effets se chargeant avec les sifflements mortels et les rauques musiques que le monde, loin derrière nous, lance sur notre mère de beauté, - elle recule, elle se dresse. Oh! nos os sont revêtus d'un nouveau corps amoureux.

O la face cendrée, l' écusson de crin, les bras de cristal! le canon sur lequel je dois m'abattre à travers la mêlée des arbres et de l'air léger!

Beautiful Being

Before the snow the Beautiful One stands tall. The whistles of death & the circles of morally dull musical fountains swell & tremble like a troop of worshiped ghosts; red & black bruises appear on the superb flesh. The colors of life itself deepen, dance, & detach from the Vision, in the shipyard. Earthquakes threaten & rumble, & the force of these effects mix with mortal sounds & the raucous music of the world, far behind, & launches our beautiful mother, - herself remote, herself still standing. Oh! Our bones are upholstered with a new body of love.

Oh the face of ash, the emblematic mane, the arms of crystal! The cannon that knocks me down in a melody of trees & song of light!

A Une Raison

Un coup de ton doigt sur le tambour décharge tous les sons et commence la nouvelle harmonie.

Un pas de toi, c'est la levée des nouveaux hommes et leur en-marche.

Ta tête se détourne: le nouvel amour!
Ta tête se retourne, - le nouvel amour

"Change nos lots, crible les fléaux, à commencer par le temps," te chantent ces enfants. "Elève n'importe où la subtance de nos fortunes et de nos voeux," on t'en prie.

Arrivée de toujours, qui t'en iras partout.

One Reason

A tap of your finger on the tambourine discharges all sound & initiates the new harmony.

One step from you, an army of fresh troops begins to march.

You turn your head: love is renewed!
Your head turns back: love is renewed!

"Save us from fate & end all our ills, from the beginning of time," the children sing. "Improve our fortunes substantially & fulfill our desires," they pray.

You will arrive in time, because you are everywhere.

Guerre

Enfant, certains ciels ont affiné mon optique: tous les caractères nuancèrent ma physionomie. Les phénomènes s'émurent. - A présent, l'inflexion éternelle des moments et l'infini des mathématiques me chassent par ce monde où je subis tous les succès civils, respecté de l'enfance étrange et des affections énormes. - Je songe à une guerre de droit ou de force, de logique bien imprévue.

C'est aussi simple qu'une phrase musicale.

War

Child, special skies have opened my eyes: the nuances of their characters shaded my own face. The phenomenon were imitated. Now, the inflection of everlasting moments & the infinity of mathematics chases me all over the world, where I've become a popular star, esteemed recipient of the respect & enormous affections of strange children. I dream of a War, of righteous might or unimagined logic.

It is as simple as a phrase of music.

Départ

Assez vu. La vision s'est rencontrée à tous les airs. Assez eu. Rumeurs des villes, le soir, et au soleil, et toujours.

Assez connu. Les arrêts de la vie. - O Rumeurs et Visions!

Départ dans l'affection et le bruit neufs!

Leaving

Seen enough. The picture was the same in every climate.
Had it all. The racket of villages, forever in the sunlight.

Knew too much. The dead ends of a life. - Oh Racket &
Visions!

Escape into love & new sounds!

Resources

Rimbaud: Complete Works, Selected Letters. Wallace Fowlie, tr. University of Chicago Press, 1966.

Rimbaud Complete. Wyatt Mason, tr. Modern Library, 2002.

I Promise To Be Good: The Letters of Arthur Rimbaud. Wyatt Mason, tr. Modern Library, 2003.

Rimbaud: Complete Works. Paul Schmidt, tr. Harper & Row, 1976.

Rimbaud. Enid Starkie. New Directions, 1957.

Rimbaud: Illuminations and Other Prose Poems. Louise Varese, tr. New Directions, 1957.

Index Of First Lines

About The Translator

Eric Greinke is a widely published poet whose poetry has appeared in many literary magazines, such as Bogg, Free Verse, Iconoclast, The New York Quarterly, The Pedestal, The University of Tampa Review & The Wilderness House Literary Review. *He has worked in Poets In The Schools, & for over twenty-five years as a social worker for disturbed & disabled children. He is the author of several collections of poetry, fiction & social commentary. Website: www.ericgreinke.com*

Check our website for other titles.
www.presapress.com